The Night before Christmas

igloo

'Twas the Night Before Christmas

'Twas the night before Christmas, when all through the house,
Not a creature was stirring, not even a mouse.
The stockings were hung by the chimney with care,
In hopes that St Nicholas soon would be there.

The children were nestled all snug in their beds,
While visions of sugar-plums danced in their heads.
And Mamma in her 'kerchief and I in my cap,
Had just settled our brains for a long winter's nap.

When out on the lawn there arose such a clatter,
I sprang from the bed to see what was the matter.
Away to the window I flew like a flash,
Tore open the shutters and threw up the sash.

The moon on the breast of the new-fallen snow,
Gave the lustre of mid-day to objects below.
When, what to my wondering eyes should appear,
But a miniature sleigh and eight tiny reindeer.

With a little old driver, so lively and quick,
I knew in a moment, it must be St Nick.
More rapid than eagles his coursers they came,
And he whistled and shouted and called them by name!

"Now Dasher! Now Dancer! Now Prancer and Vixen!
On Comet! On Cupid! On Donner and Blitzen!
To the top of the porch! To the top of the wall!
Now dash away! Dash away! Dash away all!"

Can you find the missing stickers to complete this picture?

Whose Gift?

The children can't wait to open their presents. Can you find the correct stickers for each child, to see what Santa has brought them?

What would you like Santa to bring you for Christmas? Write your list here.

Dear Santa,
for Christmas I would love...

Santa's Snacks

Santa gets hungry when he delivers all the presents. Children usually leave food and drink out for him, but this time there's only a glass of milk.

Can you draw some mince pies, or other treats on the plate and add some carrots for the reindeer?

Follow the Stars

Which star trail will lead Santa to his sack of presents?

a.

b.

c.

Guess the Gifts

Can you guess what toys Santa has in his sleigh?

a.

b.

c.

d.

e.

Join the Dots

Join the bel's to see who is pulling the sleigh.
Then decorate the picture.

34 35 2
33
32 1
31 3 4
30 5
29 23 6
17 10
28 15 11 7
16 9 8
24 18 9
22
27 25 12
26 14 13
21 19
20

Mischievous Mice

There are six mice hiding in this
picture. Can you spot them all?

Festive Fun

Help to get the house ready for Santa's arrival. Use your stickers to hang up stockings by the fireplace, leave gifts under the tree and add baubles to the tree.

Christmas Cookies

Why not make some Christmas cookies to leave out for Santa?
Always ask a grown-up to help you when you are cooking.

Ingredients:

140g, 5oz, or 1 cup icing sugar, sieved
1 tsp vanilla extract
1 egg yolk
225g, 8oz, or 1 cup butter, cut into cubes
350g, 14 oz, or 3½ cups plain flour, sieved

To decorate:

250g, 10 oz, or 2 cups icing sugar, sieved
Edible gold and silver balls
Food dye

Equipment

A mixing bowl
A wooden spoon, or electric hand mixer
2x baking trays
A wire rack
Star/Christmas tree cookie cutters
Cling film
Baking paper

Instructions:

1. Before you start, wash your hands.
2. Pre-heat the oven to 375°F, 190°C, or Gas Mark 5. Ask an adult to do this for you.
3. Line two baking trays with non-stick baking paper.
4. Put the icing sugar, vanilla extract, egg yolk and butter into a mixing bowl and beat together until the mixture is smooth.
5. Add the flour and mix to a firm dough.
6. Shape the dough into two flat discs and wrap in cling film. Put them into the refrigerator for 20 to 30 mins.
7. Roll the dough on a lightly-floured surface, until one finger thick.
8. Press out your Christmas shapes using your cutters.
9. Place on the baking trays and bake for 10 to 12 mins until lightly golden.
10. Put the cookies onto a wire rack to cool.
11. Mix the icing sugar with a few drops of cold water and food dye to make a thick, but still runny icing.
12. Spread the icing over the cooled biscuits and decorate with edible gold and silver balls.

Try not to eat them all before Santa gets to your house!

Which Way?

Help Santa deliver the gifts.
Find the missing reindeer sticker to complete the picture.
Which route leads Santa to the house with the little boy in?

a.
b.
c.

Reindeer Muddle

Look at the picture below of Dasher, Dancer,
Prancer, Vixen, Comet, Cupid, Donder and Blitzen.

Circle the reindeer that appears twice.

a.
b.
c.
d.
e.
f.
g.
h.

Santa's Sleigh

1. Fold the tab, on the picture of the presents, along the dotted line. Then push through the vertical slot on the picture of the sleigh, as shown in figure a.

2. Fold back the sleigh support, along the dotted line, so the sleigh stands up, as shown in figure b.

3. Push the locking tabs through the slots on the reindeer and fold back the leg supports, as shown in figure c.

4. Push the reigns on the sleigh through the slots on the reindeer, as shown, in figure d.

figure.a

figure.b

figure.c

figure.d

Tree Decorations

The Night Before Ch

Find the Stockings

Which Way?

Festive Fun

locking
tabs

Tree Decorations

Shade the Christmas tree using the key provided. Using your stickers, place some gifts under the tree.

- blue
- green
- red
- yellow
- black
- brown

What doesn't Belong?

Circle the things that don't belong at Christmas time.

a.

b.

c.

d.

e.

f.

g.

h.

i.

j.

Where's my Shadow?

Which shadow matches which reindeer?
Draw a line between them

l.

a.

b.

c.

1.

2.

3.

Santa Christmas Tree Decorations

You will need:
Red card
White card
Black paper
Cotton wool
Gold paper
Crayons, or felt-tip pens
Scissors (with adult supervision)
Craft glue
String, or ribbon

To make Santa

1. With the help of an adult, cut out a circle of white card, about 5cm (2in) across and draw Santa's face on to it. Don't forget his rosy cheeks.
2. Cut out a circle of red card, about 10cm (4in) across. Glue the white circle onto the top of the red circle, as shown.
3. Stick a thin strip of black paper across the red circle. This is Santa's belt.
4. Cut out a small square of gold paper to make the buckle and stick it in the middle of the belt.
5. Cut out a triangle hat-shape in red card and glue it on top of Santa's head.
6. Glue a small blob of cotton wool onto the end of the hat and more across the bottom edge.
7. Glue some cotton wool around Santa's face for a beard.
8. Punch a small hole in Santa's hat and thread through some string, or ribbon.

Now hang Santa on your Christmas tree. Why not make lots?

Find Dasher's Dinner

Help Dasher find his way through the maze to the food.

Handprint Santa Christmas Card

You will need:

Large pieces of card in bright shades
Washable water-based white paint
Washable water-based pink paint
Washable water-based red paint
Scissors (with adult supervision)
Paint brushes
Red paper
Glue
Googly eyes
A black pen

Instructions:

1. Fold your large piece of card in half to make a greeting card.

2. Cut a jacket shape out of red paper and stick onto the card, as shown.

3. Cut a Santa hat shape out of red paper. Stick the hat above the jacket, leaving a gap of about 5cm (2 inches).

4. Mix together some pink and white paint to make a light pink shade and paint a circle between the hat and the jacket. This is Santa's face.

Reindeer Food

5. Wait for the face to dry and then with a large paint brush, paint white paint directly onto the palm of your hand and your fingers.

6. Make a handprint on the front of your card. Your fingers should be facing down towards the bottom of the card. This will be Santa's beard. Now wash your hands!

7. Paint two pink circles for rosy cheeks onto Santa's face with a small paint brush. Paint one red circle for the nose and stick on two googly eyes.

8. Dip your little finger in white paint and press down each side of Santa's face. This is his hair.

9. Put white circles of paint along the edge of the hat for fur and one white circle for the hat's bobble.

Now write your message inside and send it to someone special.

to sam,

Happy Christmas

love from Jo xxx

Fairy Light Fun

Shade the fairy lights so that they follow the correct pattern.

Which Chimney?

Climbing down chimneys is a dangerous job.
Help Santa decide which chimneys to go down and which to avoid.

a.   b.   c.

Find the Stockings

The stockings are missing.
Find the stickers of the missing stockings by following the clues.

This stocking belongs to one of Santa's helpers.

This stocking belongs to a little girl.

This stocking belongs to one of the reindeers.

This stocking belongs to a little boy.

e.

f.

g.

Santa's Sleigh Ride Game

Can you help Santa fly his sleigh around the village and deliver the presents?

Each player chooses a different Santa, or reindeer sticker, from the book and sticks it onto a coin. This will be your playing piece and should be placed on the 'START' circle. Then take it in turns to roll the dice and move round the board. The first to the sleigh wins.

START

1

2

9

8

7
You stop to deliver presents. Miss a go.

6

5

4

3

10

11

12

13

14

15

22
The reindeer are going super fast. Go forward 2 spaces.

23

24

25

26
You stop to feed your reindeer. Go back 1 space

27

21

20

19

FINISH

29

28

16
Someone has left some mince pies out for you. Go back 2 spaces.

17

18